DENNIS BEATS EVERYTHING

when it comes to drumming up funny business. Mirth, mayhem and mischief follow wherever he goes. And he goes everywhere!

It all started back in 1951 when a pint-sized, pug-nosed bundle of mischief leaped from Hank Ketcham's drawing board. He was Dennis the Menace, of course; and he's kept Hank Ketcham working for him — and America laughing — ever since.

Now here is DENNIS THE MENACE: HOUSEHOLD HURRICANE — more hilarious adventures with America's favorite little guy. It's Dennis at his menacing best.

Dennis the Menace
Household Hurricane

by Hank Ketcham

A FAWCETT CREST BOOK

Fawcett Publications, Inc., Greenwich, Conn.
Member of American Book Publishers Council, Inc.

A Fawcett Crest Book reprinted by arrangement with Holt, Rinehart
and Winston, Inc. in association with Hall Editions, Inc.

Copyright,©, 1957, by The Hall Syndicate, Inc.
Copyright, ©, 1963, 1958, 1957 by Hank Ketcham.
All rights reserved, including the right to reproduce this
book or portions thereof.

DENNIS THE MENACE, HOUSEHOLD HURRICANE was originally
published by Holt, Rinehart and Winston, Inc. This expanded
edition, prepared especially for Fawcett Publications, Inc.,
contains 62 cartoons which did not appear in the original,
higher-priced edition.

Third Fawcett Crest printing, January 1967

Published by Fawcett World Library,
67 West 44th Street, New York, N. Y. 10036.
Printed in the United States of America.

"LOOK AT ALL THE PRETTY THINGS MR. WILSON PLANTED IN HIS GARDEN!"

"IT'S GONNA BE YOUR FAULT IF I GET SHOT IN THE BACK!"

"I'M NOT IN THE MOOD FOR A BATH!"

".... AN' SO, 'TIL TOMORROW NIGHT, SAME TIME, SAME PLACE, THIS IS DENNIS SAYIN' 'AMEN'."

"DON'T IT, DAD? DON'T THAT OL' EGG LOOK LIKE A
BIG YELLOW EYE STARIN' AT YA?"

"OH-OH! SHE'S LETTING HIM LOOSE AGAIN!"

"DON'T THANK ME, THANK MRS. WILSON. SHE *GREW* 'EM. I JUST PICK 'EM."

"THERE. NOW WE'LL LET IT DRY FOR A COUPLE MINUTES..."

"I GOT WHAT *I* WANT, BUT RUFF'S STILL TRYIN' TO MAKE UP HIS MIND."

"EVER NOTICE HOW HIS TONGUE FALLS OUT WHEN HE GETS HOT?"

"WE'RE PLAYIN' FIREMAN. YOU'RE THE HOUSE!"

"WE'RE ALL GOIN' TO THE BEACH! WANNA DRIVE?"

"HURRY UP AN' GIVE US THE TICKET!
I GOTTA GO TO THE BATHROOM!"

"BUT *WHY*? WHY? *WHY* WOULD HE PUT AN ONION IN MY LINGERIE DRAWER?"

"I'M NOT GONNA USE YOU FOR A MOTHER NO MORE!"

"YA DARN *RIGHT* I'M SICK! I'M SICK OF KINDERGARTER, I'M SICK OF WASHIN', I'M SICK OF LIVER . . . ."

"YOU KEEP ON POKIN' ME IN MY STOMACH AN' YOU'RE
GONNA FEEL BAD, TOO!"

"COME ON, SONNY. GIVE ME MY CAP. WON'T YOU EVEN ROLL DOWN THE WINDOW, SONNY? OR UNLOCK THE DOOR? SONNY? *LISTEN, KID!...*"

"WE WANT THE ONES WITH THE LITTLEST HOLES!"

"HERE! YOU GET SOME MORE WATER! I'LL GO BACK AN' PICK UP THE FISH!"

"HOW 'BOUT WHEN I RAN THROUGH MR. WILSON'S SPRINKLER... DON'T THAT COUNT AS A BATH?"

"I DIDN'T SAY I WANTED A DRINK.
I SAID I NEEDED SOME WATER!"

"IF I WAS A BURGLAR, YOU'D BE IN TROUBLE. YOU LEFT YOUR FRONT DOOR OPEN!"

"HOW COME HE SNEAKS OUT EVERY MORNING AND LEAVES YOU WITH ALL THE WORK?"

"SEE? I *TOLD* YOU THIS WOULD HAPPEN
WHEN YA BOUGHT THE THING!"

"WATCH ME WEIGH A HUNDRED POUNDS!"

"LET'S NOT TELL DAD, MOM. IT'LL JUST SPOIL HIS WHOLE EVENING. OKAY, MOM? MOM?"

"YOU GUESS YOUR GRANDPA WOULD CARE IF WE FILLED IT WITH DRY GRASS AND USED IT FOR A TARGET?"

"HOW 'BOUT ME? I HAD A TOUGH DAY IN THE BACK YARD!"

"THERE, THERE, HONEY. DON'T CRY. *DENNIS*, HOW DID YOUR *SHOE* GET IN THE CEREAL?"

"YOU GOT ANY KIDS MY AGE?"

"HANG ON *TIGHT*, LADY! I'M TAKIN' THIS STAGECOACH TO TEXAS!"

"WOULD YA CUT THAT HAIR AROUND HIS MOUTH? IT GETS IN HIS MILK."

"GET THE SOAP, MR. RAGAN! HE SAID IT AGAIN!"

"I BET EVERYTHING DIDN'T GO JUST PERFECT THE FIRST TIME *YOU* EVER TOOK A SHOWER EITHER!"

"WHEN DOES SHE THINK SHE'S GONNA GET TIME TO *READ?*"

"...AND WHEN THESE BIG OL' UGLY, HAIRY SPACE MEN
GRABBED THE BABY SITTER...."

"SEE? *THAT'S* THE WAY TO SCARE A DOG CATCHER!"

"MOM! WOULD YOU COME IN HERE
AN' READ SOMETHIN' FOR ME?"

"I'M NOT GONNA PICK UP MY TOYS UNTIL I GET GOOD AND..... JOKE! THAT'S A JOKE, DAD!"

"... AN' IF THEY DON'T SEE THE SIGN, THEY WON'T BUY YOUR HOUSE, AN' YOU WON'T HAVE TO MOVE. RIGHT?"

"I'M NOT HIDING *ANYTHING!* I'M STUFFING OUR TURKEY!"

"BEFORE YOU GET MAD... AREN'T YOU PROUD THAT I CAN KICK A FOOTBALL ALL THE WAY FROM OUR YARD TO MISTER WILSON'S WINDOW?"

"AREN'T YOU A LITTLE BIG TO BE ROCKED?"

"It was easy. I made a rope out of your neckties!"

"WHAT'S THE MATTER WITH YOU, DENNIS? I WASN'T EVEN *NEAR* YOUR PIGGY BANK!"

"AND WHAT IF I'M *NOT* OUT OF TOWN BY SUNDOWN?"

"I DON'T SEE NO BLUE STREAK WHEN SHE TALKS!"

" 'LISTEN, FOLKS, I'M NOT GONNA GO TO BED 'TIL I
GET GOOD 'N' READY!' *THAT'S* WHAT I SHOULDA SAID!"

"GO ON, *TRY* ME! YOU NAME THE CAR, I'LL SING THE COMMERCIAL!"

"HAVE YOU SEEN A LADY WITHOUT A LITTLE KID WHO LOOKS LIKE ME?"

"WHAT CAN SHE DO WITH FLOWERS? SHE COULD *EAT* CANDY!"

"*TWELVE* TIMES! I'VE KEPT TRACK."

"I OILED THE PIANO WITHOUT ANYBODY EVEN ASKING ME TO DO IT!"

"... AND STOP WHISTLING AT ME!"

"HOW CAN I 'HAVE FUN'? I CAN'T HARDLY *MOVE!*"

"YOU *SURE* HE TRIED TO CUT OFF YOUR EAR, SONNY? THEY BOTH LOOK OKAY TO ME."

"I *THOUGHT* I HEARD SOMEBODY CRUNCHIN' POTATO CHIPS!"

*"NEXT TIME YOU SEE DAD, *BITE* 'IM!"

"LET'S TURN THE PAGE! I'M *TIRED* OF LOOKIN' AT THAT OL' GIRL!"

"YOU'RE SUPPOSED TO GO TO SLEEP. THAT WAS *TAPS!*"

"I DON'T UNDERSTAND IT. *I'M* THE QUIET TYPE, *YOU'RE* THE QUIET TYPE ....."

"SEE? DON'T THAT LOOK LIKE PURE WHITE SAND?"

"DID YOU EVER EVEN *HEAR* OF A COWBOY SLEEPIN' IN PAJAMAS? HUH? DID YA? HUH?"

"I'LL BET THAT OL' FLY WON'T BOTHER *ME* AGAIN! HERE'S YOUR PAPER, DAD."

"THIS IS THE COOKHOUSE, AND THAT'S MY COOK, NOW FOLLOW ME AN' I'LL SHOW YA MY BUNKHOUSE."

"TOMORROW'S MOTHER'S DAY, MOM! SO I'M GONNA SPEND *ALL DAY* PLAYIN' WITH YOU!"

"AW, MOM! YOU DON'T LOOK LIKE A MOTHER IN THEM THINGS!"

"A YO-YO IN MY *WHAT?*"

"I HAVE *PLENTY* OF TIME TO MAKE A PIE BEFORE DINNER! NOW TURN THAT TELEVISION BACK ON BEFORE I GET MAD!"

"HI, MOM! I WAS LOOKIN' FOR YA!"

"I'LL JUST *DIE* IF MY PERMANENT TEETH AREN'T PRETTY!"

"OH, DEAR! YOUR FATHER SURE ISN'T THE TYPE FOR BATHING SUITS, IS HE?"

"HEY, THE TELEBISHION ISN'T BROKE!
IT ISN'T PLUGGED *IN!*"

"TELL ME THE TRUTH... WOULD YOU MARRY A GIRL WHO WORE GLASSES?"

"NOT SO *HARD!* I WON'T HAVE NO FINGERPRINTS LEFT!"

"IT DON'T SMELL HALF AS GOOD AS PEANUT BUTTER!"

"DID YA GET A CHANCE TO COUNT ALL THAT MONEY YET?"

"YOU CAN DROP YOUR HANDS, SONNY. THIS IS JUST A
PARKING TICKET."

"YOU WEREN'T HOME SO WE GOT OUR OWN DINNER."

"YOU'RE LUCKY! THE GOOD FAIRY WILL GIVE YA TWO BITS FOR THAT TOOTH I KNOCKED OUT IF YOU'LL PUT IT UNDER YOUR PILLOW."

"EVER SEE SUCH NERVOUS PEOPLE?"

"COME ON IN! MY FOLKS *LOVE* MUSIC!"

"WE ALL GO OVER TO MY HOUSE, SEE? AND MY DAD GIVES US A NICKEL TO PLAY SOMEWHERE ELSE. THEN WE ALL GO OVER TO LARRY'S...."

"I *TOLD* YA THE FAT GUY WOULD HAVE PIE!"

"THERE'S NO BURIED TREASURE IN *YOUR* BACK YARD!"

"IF THAT'S MR. WILSON . . . . IT'S NOT TRUE!"

"DON'T THINK OF IT AS MILK. THINK OF IT AS PINK CHEEKS, PRETTY TEETH AND NICE, STRAIGHT LEGS."

"WHAT'S A DATE, MOM? I GOT ONE WITH MARGARET THIS AFTERNOON."

"YOU KNOW WHY HE DON'T TALK SO GOOD? HE'S GOT THE MUMPS."

"POOR OL' RUFF FEELS LEFT OUT."

"HENRY! WILL YOU COME UP HERE? WE'VE GOT A BATHTUB FULL OF FROGS!"

"CHASIN' A FLY. WHY?"

"DON'T GET EXCITED, MOM. I'LL JUST GO AROUND ONCE!"

"C'MON! C'MON! YOU DON'T HAFTA *DROWN* YOURSELF!"

"BOY! DON'T SOME PEOPLE BUY SOME *FUNNY* LOOKIN' DOGS?"

"GEE WHIZ! SEEMS LIKE EVERYTHING I DO MAKES YOU MAD!"

"DENNIS GAVE ME A PENNY TO TAKE HIS PLACE, MRS. MITCHELL."

"YOO HOO! I'M BACK!"

"I'LL BET IT WAS THAT SMELLY OL' PIPE!"

"IF THEY TAKE YA TO THE HOSPITAL,
CAN I BLOW THE SIREN?"

"BOY, I THOUGHT DAD'S PIPE SMELLED AWFUL, BUT <u>YOURS</u> REALLY......"

"DO YOU HAVE TO SHOW HER MY ROOM WHILE I'M COUNTIN' MY MONEY?"

"WHAT A DUMB DEAL! ALL MY MONEY FOR THIS LITTLE OL' BOOK!"

"WHY NOT? YOU TOOK A PITCHER OF *ME* TAKIN' A BATH!"

"I THINK MR. WILSON IS *REALLY* GONNA SUE US *THIS* TIME!"

"YOU MUST HAVE THE WRONG NUMBER. OUR LITTLE BOY WOULDN'T BREAK WINDOWS."

"I STILL SAY IT WAS A MEAN TRICK TO SMACK ME WITH MY OWN PINGPONG PADDLE!"

"YOU GO AHEAD AND SLEEP. I'LL FIND SOME NICE NEIGHBOR LADY WHO'LL FIX ME SOME BREAKFAST."

"ASK *ME* SOMETHIN', MOM. *I'LL* TALK TO YA!"

"GOT ANY LUMP SUGAR? YA NEVER KNOW
WHEN I MIGHT MEET A HORSE!"

"IT WASN'T EASY!

"WHEN YOU READ WHAT THE LITTLE BEAR SAYS, YOU'RE SUPPOSED TO SAY IT IN A REAL HIGH, SQUEAKY VOICE!"

"WHAT? YOU MEAN YOU CAN'T SMELL THAT POPCORN?"

"CAN I LOOK UNDER YOUR SEAT? I'M LOOKIN'
FOR SOMETHIN' OF MINE THAT CRAWLED AWAY!"

"ONCE UPON A TIME THERE WAS THREE DOGS.
A PAPA DOG, A MAMA DOG, AND A BABY DOG....."

"FRANKLY, I DON'T BELIEVE A FIVE-YEAR-OLD COULD DREAM UP THE STUNTS HE PULLS. I THINK HE'S A *MIDGET!*"

"BETTER GET A *BIG* BOOK! IT'S RAININ' CATS 'N' DOGS!"

"I'VE BEEN PLAYIN' WITH MR. BRANDT DOWN AT THE POSTOFFICE ALL AFTERNOON."

"HE'S SUCH AN AFFECTIONATE KID WHY DO FOLKS CALL HIM DENNIS THE MENACE?"

"IT WOULDN'T BE SO TERRIBLE IF ONE OF YOUR RUBBER BOOTS HAD A LITTLE HOLE IN IT, WOULD IT?"

"DON'T PUT THAT SOAP IN HERE!
YA WANNA MAKE MY TURTLE SICK?"

"...AND MAKE ME A GOOD BOY. OR BETTER, ANYWAY."

"I WISH DADDY WOULD HURRY AND GO TO WORK SO
YOU AN' ME CAN GO BACK TO BED AGAIN!"